Jackie Robinson
and the Big Game

written by
Dan Gutman

illustrated by
Elaine Garvin

Aladdin

New York   London   Toronto   Sydney

To my brother Jack
—E. G.

ALADDIN PAPERBACKS

An imprint of Simon & Schuster Children's Publishing Division

1230 Avenue of the Americas

New York, NY 10020

Text copyright © 2006 by Dan Gutman

Illustrations copyright © 2006 by Elaine Garvin

All rights reserved, including the right of

reproduction in whole or in part in any form.

READY-TO-READ is a registered trademark of Simon & Schuster, Inc.

ALADDIN PAPERBACKS, CHILDHOOD OF FAMOUS AMERICANS,

and colophon are trademarks of Simon & Schuster, Inc.

Designed by Lisa Vega

The text of this book was set in 18-Point Century Old Style.

Manufactured in the United States of America

First Aladdin Paperbacks edition January 2006

4 6 8 10 9 7 5 3

Library of Congress Cataloging-in-Publication Data

Gutman, Dan.

Jackie Robinson and the big game / by Dan Gutman; illustrated by Elaine Garvin.

p. cm.—(Ready-to-read childhood of famous Americans)

Summary: Presents the childhood of the man who would grow up to

be the first African American player in major league baseball.

ISBN 13: 978-0-689-86239-7—ISBN 10: 0-689-86239-3 (pbk.)

ISBN 13: 978-0-689-86240-3—ISBN 10: 0-689-86240-7 (library ed.)

1. Robinson, Jackie, 1919–1972—Childhood and youth—Juvenile literature.

2. Baseball players—United States—Biography—Juvenile literature.

[1. Robinson, Jackie, 1919–1972—Childhood and youth. 2. Baseball players.

3. African Americans—Biography.] I. Garvin, Elaine, ill. II. Title.

III. Series: Ready-to-read childhood of the famous Americans.

GV865.R6G88 2005

796.357'092—dc21

2002155969

Jackie Robinson
and the Big Game

Plick! Plock!

The little white ball

zipped back and forth.

PASADENA YOUTH TABLE
TENNIS TOURNAMENT.
TEN DOLLAR GRAND PRIZE.

"I bet I could win,"
  nine-year-old Jackie Robinson
  told his friends.

"Jackie, you never played
  Ping-Pong in your life!"

"How hard could it be?"
  Jackie asked.

Jackie watched carefully,

and learned very fast.

He beat everyone in the contest!

By the end of the morning

he had become

the best Ping-Pong player

in Pasadena, California.

Jackie ran home for lunch.
He gave the money he won
to his mother.

9

Jackie's brothers and sister
admired his trophy.

"Nice," his brother Mack said,
"but you can't run
as fast as me."

Jackie could never

turn down a dare.

But Mack was fourteen.

He was bigger and stronger.

He beat Jackie easily

every time.

After lunch

the kids on Pepper Street

played Chase the Fox.

They would link arms
and try to prevent
the kid in the middle
from running away.
Mack was the fastest fox.
Nobody could catch him.

"Let's see who can jump
the farthest," Mack said
as he and Jackie walked home.
"Let's see who can hit
that tree with a rock."

No matter what game they played,
Mack always won.

Jackie didn't like to lose.

He ran home, stomped

upstairs, slammed his bedroom door,

and ripped Mack's shoes!

Jackie's mother was angry when she
saw the shoes. But she knew how
much her youngest son hated to lose.

"One day you will be as big
as Mack," she told Jackie.
"You will be better than him
at something."
But Jackie didn't think he would
ever beat Mack at anything.

"Hey, Jackie! Want to play?"
Mack and his friends were playing
baseball in the park.

"No thanks,"
Jackie said.
"I don't know how to play baseball."

"Come on!" one of the boys yelled.
"Grab a bat."

Jackie stepped up to the plate.

Mack threw him a pitch.

Jackie smashed the ball

right back at Mack.

At first base, Jackie
watched his brother carefully.
When Mack threw the next pitch,
Jackie ran.

He slid into second base

in a cloud of dust.

Safe!

On the next pitch

Jackie stole third base.

"Don't even THINK
about stealing home on me,"
Mack yelled to his brother.

"Oh, I'm thinking about it,"
Jackie yelled back.
As soon as Mack
got ready to pitch, Jackie took
off from third base.

It was a race to the plate.

The catcher caught the ball.

Jackie slid in hard.

He knocked the ball

out of the catcher's mitt.

Safe again!

Soon it was too dark
to play anymore.
"You're pretty good at
baseball, Jackie,"
Mack said as they walked home.
"I thought you said
you didn't know how to play?

"How hard could it be?"
Jackie asked.

When he grew up, Jackie Robinson became the first African American in sixty years to play major league baseball. Mack Robinson won two Olympic medals. The friendly competition they had as children helped make both brothers into stars.

Here is a timeline of Jackie's life:

1914 Mack Robinson born in Cairo, Georgia

1919 Jackie Roosevelt Robinson born on January 31 in Cairo, Georgia

1936 Mack wins two medals in track and field at the Olympics in Berlin, Germany. He finishes second in the 200-meter sprint behind Jesse Owens

1939 Jackie is a football, baseball, and track star at UCLA

1941 The United States enters World War II. Jackie enlists in the U.S. Army

1947 Jackie plays his first game for the Brooklyn Dodgers. They win the National League pennant. Jackie is named Rookie of the Year

1949 Jackie wins the Most Valuable Player Award. The Dodgers win the pennant

1955 The Dodgers win the pennant again, and go on to win their first and only World Series

1956 The Dodgers win the pennant for the sixth time in Jackie's career. He retires from baseball and begins a career as a businessman and civil rights activist

1962 Jackie is inducted into National Baseball Hall of Fame

1972 Jackie dies on October 24